TANNISHO

A Shin Buddhist Classic

As translated by
Taitetsu Unno

Buddhist Study Center Press
Honolulu, Hawaii

Library of Congress Cataloging-in-Publication Data
Shinran, 1173 – 1263.
   [Tannishō. English]
   Tannisho: a Shin Buddhist classic / as translated by Taitetsu
Unno. — Rev. ed.
      p.   cm.
   Includes bibliographical references.
   ISBN 0-938474-18-9
   1.   Shin (Sect) — Doctrines — Early works to 1800.   I. Unno,
Taitetsu, 1929 –   . II. Title.
BQ8749.S554T3513   1996
294.3'85 — dc20   96-12400
                                           CIP

Cover by Lori Oumaye.
Printed by Thomson-Shore, Inc., Dexter, Michigan.

FOREWORD
To the Second Revised Edition

This is a completely revised version of my *Tannisho: A Shin Buddhist Classic*, published in 1984, which was based upon an earlier work, *Tannisho: Lamenting the Deviations* (1977).

This work contains the sayings of Shinran (1173-1263), the founder of Jodo Shinshu or Shin Buddhism, which claims the largest following in Japanese Buddhism. Compiled several decades after his death by a disciple named Yui-en, this work consists of 18 sections. The first ten sections are the words of Shinran as remembered by Yui-en, and the next eight, preceded by a special preface, contains points of controversy current among the followers of Shinran. The prologue and epilogue to the 18 sections were written by Yui-en about whom little is known historically.

The *Tannisho* is one of the most widely read works in Japanese Buddhism, known not only as a religious but literary classic. It is impossible to translate such a work into English adequately and fully, but I have attempted to transmit some sense of its flowing style, religious content, and spiritual flavor. Among those who have guided me in my enterprise, I should like to gratefully acknowledge the comments and suggestions offered by two late teachers, Yoshifumi Ueda and Masao Hanada, whose words remain a constant source of inspiration.

Taitetsu Unno
Northampton, Massachusetts
January 1, 1996

TABLE OF CONTENTS

English Translation of

TANNISHO

PROLOGUE

In reflecting upon my foolish thoughts and thinking of the past and present, I deeply regret that there are views deviating from the true entrusting *(shinjin)* which was taught orally by our late master, and I fear that doubts and confusions may arise among the followers who come after us. Unless we rely upon a good teacher with whom our karmic destinies are fortunately bound, how can we possibly enter the gate of effortless practice? Do not violate the fundamentals of Other Power by imposing upon it your own interpretations.

Thus have I committed to writing some words of the late Shinran which still ring clearly in my ears. My sole purpose is to dispel the clouds of doubt in the minds of the practicers with the same aspiration.

with "shinjin"

I

When the thought of saying the nembutsu erupts from deep within, having entrusted ourselves to the inconceivable power of Amida's vow which saves us, enabling us to be born in the Pure Land, we receive at that very moment the ultimate benefit of being grasped never to be abandoned.

Amida's Primal Vow does not discriminate between the young and old, good and evil — true entrusting alone is essential. The reason is that the Vow is directed to the person burdened with the weight of karmic evil and burning with the flames of blind passion.

Thus, in entrusting ourselves to the Primal Vow, no other form of good is necessary, for there is no good that surpasses the nembutsu. And evil need not be feared, for there is no evil which can obstruct the working of Amida's Primal Vow.

II

I believe that the reason you have come here, crossing over more than ten provinces at the risk of your lives, is solely to ascertain the path that leads to birth in the Pure Land. But if you suspect that I know ways other than the nembutsu to attain birth, or that I am versed in the scriptures connected with them, you are greatly mistaken. If that be the case, there are many eminent scholars in the monasteries of Nara and Mt. Hiei, so you should go see them and ask them in detail about the way to attain birth in the Pure Land.

As for myself, Shinran, I simply take to heart the words of my dear teacher, Honen, "Just say the nembutsu and be saved by Amida," and entrust myself to the Primal Vow. Besides this, there is nothing else.

I really do not know whether the nembutsu may be the cause for my birth in the Pure Land, or the act that shall condemn me to hell. But I have nothing to regret, even if I should have been deceived by my teacher, and, saying the nembutsu, fall into hell. The reason is that if I were capable of realizing buddhahood by other religious practices and yet fell into hell for saying the nembutsu, I might have dire regrets for having been deceived. But since I am absolutely incapable of any religious practice, hell is my only home.

If Amida's Primal Vow is true, Sakyamuni's teaching cannot be false. If the Buddha's teaching is true, Shan-tao's commentaries cannot be false. If Shan-tao's commentaries are true, how can Honen's words be empty of meaning? If Honen's words are true, what I, Shinran, say cannot be meaningless. In brief, such is the true entrusting of this foolish one. Now, whether you accept the nembutsu, entrusting yourself to it, or reject it, that is your own decision.

III

Even the good person attains birth in the Pure Land, how much more so the evil person.

But the people of the world constantly say, even the evil person attains birth, how much more so the good person. Although this appears to be sound at first glance, it goes against the intention of the Primal Vow of Other Power. The reason is that since the person of self-power, being conscious of doing good, lacks the thought of entrusting the self completely to Other Power, he or she is not the focus of the Primal Vow of Amida. But when self-power is turned over and entrusting to Other Power occurs, the person attains birth in the land of True Fulfillment.

The Primal Vow was established out of deep compassion for us who cannot become freed from the bondage of birth-and-death through any religious practice, due to the abundance of blind passion. Since its basic intention is to effect the enlightenment of such an evil one, the evil person who is led to true entrusting by Other Power is the person who attains birth in the Pure Land. Thus, even the good person attains birth, how much more so the evil person!

IV

There is a difference in compassion between the Path of Sages and the Path of Pure Land. The compassion in the Path of Sages is expressed through pity, sympathy, and care for all beings, but rare is it that one can help another as completely as one desires.

The compassion in the Path of Pure Land is to quickly attain Buddhahood, saying the nembutsu, and with the true heart of compassion and love save all beings completely as we desire.

In this life no matter how much pity and sympathy we may feel for others, it is impossible to help another as we truly wish; thus our compassion is inconsistent and limited. Only the saying of nembutsu manifests the complete and never ending compassion which is true, real, and sincere.

Argument of Buddhism in P.L.

V

I, Shinran, have never even once uttered the nembutsu for the sake of my father and mother. The reason is that all beings have been fathers and mothers, brothers and sisters, in the timeless process of birth-and-death. When I attain buddhahood in the next birth, each and everyone will be saved.

If it were a good accomplished by my own powers, then I could transfer the accumulated merits of nembutsu to save my father and mother. But since such is not the case, when we become free from self-power and quickly attain the enlightenment of the Pure Land, we will save those bound closest to us through transcendental powers, no matter how deeply they are immersed in the karmic sufferings of the six realms and four modes of birth.

Can't help others because not Buddha/saṃsāra, have to achieve first.

⊛ against idea of Buddhist practices for other people, merit transfer

· Notion of self power, working against other / faith power (false)

$$\boxed{\text{VI}}$$

It is utterly unthinkable that among the followers of single-hearted nembutsu practice there are arguments about "my disciples" and "others' disciples."

As for myself, Shinran, I do not have a single disciple. If I could make others say the nembutsu through my own devices, they would be my disciples. But how arrogant it is to claim as disciples those who live the nembutsu through the sole working of Amida's compassion.

If the karmic condition for us is to come together, we shall be together; but if the karmic condition for us is to be separated, we shall be separated. How absurd it is that some people assert that if one goes against a teacher and says the nembutsu under another, that person cannot attain birth in the Pure Land. Are they saying that they will take back the entrusting which is a gift from Amida as if it belonged to them? Impossible is it that such a thing should happen.

When we live according to the truth of "made to become so by itself," we shall know gratitude to the Buddha and to our teachers.

VII

In the person of nembutsu opens up the great path of unobstructed freedom. The reason is that the gods of heaven and earth bow before the practicer of true entrusting, and those of the world of demons and rival ways cannot obstruct such a person. The consequences of karmic evil cannot bear fruit, nor does any form of good equal the nembutsu. Thus, it is called the great path of unobstructed freedom.

VIII

The saying of nembutsu is neither a religious practice nor a good act. Since it is practiced without any calculation, it is "non-practice." Since it is also not a good created by my calculation, it is "non-good." Since it is nothing but Other Power, completely free of self-power, it is neither a religious practice nor a good act on the part of the practicer.

IX

"Although I say the nembutsu, I rarely experience joyful happiness nor do I have the desire to immediately go to the Pure Land. What should be done about this?" I asked. Then he responded, "I, Shinran, have been having the same question also, and now you, Yui-en, have the same thought."

"When I carefully consider the matter, my birth in the Pure land is settled without doubt for the very reason that I do not rejoice about that which I should be bursting with joy. It is the working of blind passion which suppresses the heart that would rejoice and prevents its fullest expression. All this the Buddha already knew and called us foolish beings filled with blind passion. Thus, when we realize that the compassionate Vow of Other Power is for beings like ourselves, the Vow becomes even more reliable and dependable."

"The working of blind passion also causes us not to want to go to the Pure land and makes us feel uneasy worrying about death when we become even slightly ill. Impossible it seems to leave this old house of agitation where we have wandered aimlessly since the beginning of time, nor can we long for the Pure Land of peace which we have yet to know. This is due to blind passion so truly powerful and overwhelming. But no matter how reluctant we may be, when our life in this world comes to an end, beyond our control, then for the first time we go to the land of Fulfillment. Those who do not want to go immediately are the special concern of true compassion. For this very reason the Vow of true compassion is completely dependable, and our birth in the Pure Land is absolutely certain."

"If our hearts were filled with joyful happiness and we desired to go swiftly to the Pure Land, we might be misled to think that perhaps we are free of blind passion."

Blind passion = being saved, further proves amit-this vows

The Master Shinran said, "In the nembutsu no self-working is true-working; it is beyond description, explanation, and conception."

SPECIAL PREFACE

While the master was still living, those who journeyed together with great difficulty to the distant capital with the same aspiration and who, unified in true entrusting, set their hearts on the coming land of Fulfillment, all listened at the same time to his real thoughts. But now I hear that among the countless young and old people who live the nembutsu, following after them, there are some who frequently express erroneous views never taught by our master. Such groundless views call for careful discussion which follows.

XI

In meeting unlettered people who say the nembutsu some people disturb them with such questions as, "Do you say the nembutsu by entrusting yourself to the inconceivable power of the Vow or to the inconceivable power of the Name?" They fail to clarify the two forms of inconceivable powers and their respective significance. Thus, they confuse the people. We must turn our attention to this matter and carefully consider the connection between the two.

By virtue of the inconceivable power of the Vow, Amida Buddha devised the Name easy to uphold and pronounce and, thereby, promised to take in all who say the Name. Thus, when we entrust ourselves to the inconceivable power of Amida's compassionate vow which saves us to deliver us from birth-and-death and when we realize that the saying of nembutsu occurs because of Tathagata's working, we are in accord with the Primal Vow and will be born in the land of Fulfillment, since our own calculation is not involved.

When we entrust ourselves completely to the inconceivable power of the Primal Vow as the heart of the matter, then the inconceivable power of the Name is also naturally found together with it. The inconceivable powers of the Vow and of the Name are therefore one, the slightest difference between the two being non-existent.

Next, the person who inserts his or her own calculations into the consideration of good and evil, believing that the former helps and the latter hinders birth in the Pure Land, fails to entrust the self to the inconceivable power of the Vow. Rather, such a person strives with effort to achieve birth, claiming the nembutsu uttered as one's own practice. The person also fails to entrust the self to the inconceivable power of the Name.

However, even though the person fails to entrust the self, he or she will be born in the borderland, the realm of indolence, the castle of doubt, or the palace of womb to be eventually born in the land of Fulfillment by virtue of the Vow which vowed that unless all beings are saved, Amida will not have attained Buddhahood. All this is due to the inconceivable power of the Name. Since this is also due to the inconceivable power of the Vow, the Vow and the Name are one and the same.

XII

Some people say that those who do not read and study the sutras and commentaries cannot be ascertained of birth in the Pure Land. This view is hardly worthy of serious consideration.

All the sutras which reveal the essentials of the truth of Other Power simply state: By saying the nembutsu, entrusting oneself to the Primal Vow, one attains buddhahood. What further knowledge is required for birth in the Pure Land? Truly, those who are still confused about this should by all means study hard to realize the purpose of the Primal Vow. If the true meaning of the sacred texts is not clearly understood, even though one reads and studies, it is to be pitied.

Since the Name is devised to be easily said by the unlettered who cannot even grasp the basic meaning of the sutras and commentaries, such utterance is called easy practice. Learning is required in the Path of Sages; therefore, it is called difficult practice. Some people mistakenly pursue knowledge for the sake of fame and profit — their birth in the next life is doubtful, so states an attesting passage.

Today, the people of single-hearted nembutsu and those of the Path of Sages engage in argument, claiming that one school is superior and the other inferior. Thus, enemies of dharma appear and slandering of dharma becomes rampant. But does this not slander and destroy one's own teaching?

Even if all the other schools together proclaim, "The nembutsu is for foolish beings; its teaching is shallow and vulgar," you should not object. And instead simply reply, "We are taught that foolish beings *more reference to Mappo, only way to be saved*

of inferior capacity like ourselves, unlettered and ignorant, will be saved by entrusting ourselves to Amida. As we accept this and entrust ourselves, it is the supreme dharma for us, regardless of how vulgar it may seem to people of superior capacity. No matter how superb other teachings may be, if they are beyond our grasp and mastery, we cannot uphold them. Since it is the basic intention of the Buddhas that we shall all together go beyond birth-and-death, you should not hinder us." In this way, if we have no rancor, who would want to hurt us? An attesting passage also states, "Where there are arguments, various kinds of blind passion are awakened; the wise should avoid them."

The late master also said, "The Buddha predicted that there will be people who shall entrust themselves to this dharma, as well as those who shall slander it. I have already been made to entrust myself to the dharma, while there are those who slander it — by this we know that the Buddha's words are true. In fact, we should realize that our birth is even more firmly settled. If, contrary to this, no one denounced the nembutsu, we might wonder why even though there are believers, there are no slanderers. But this, of course, does not mean that the teaching should become the object of slander. The Buddha taught this because he knew that both believers and slanderers would exist. It was to dispel any doubts that might arise among us.

Is the only purpose of knowledge to defend against criticism and to engage in arguments and debates? If a person studies properly, he or she will come to see more clearly the intention of the Buddha and realize the boundlessness of true compassion. Such a student will teach those who are unsure of birth in the Pure Land because of their defiled nature that the Primal vow does not discriminate between the good and evil, the pure and impure. Only then will knowledge be meaningful.

People who insist that knowledge is essential for the religious life frighten those who live the nembutsu according to the Primal Vow. Such pedagogues are demons who obstruct the dharma, and they are despised enemies of the Buddha. They not only lack the true entrusting to Other Power but wrongly mislead other people. They should stand in fear lest they go against the teaching of our late master. And they should be filled with remorse for going against the Primal Vow.

XIII

Some people say that those who do not fear committing evil because of the inconceivable power of Amida's Vow are guilty of taking pride in the Primal Vow and, therefore, will not attain birth. This betrays doubt in the Primal Vow and shows a lack of understanding of good and evil as the product of past karma.

Good thoughts arise in our minds due to the effect of past good, and we are made to think and do evil because of the working of karmic evil. The late master said, "We should know that even as trifling a thing as the speck of dust on the tip of a rabbit's hair or a sheep's fleece is the product of past evil karma." At another time he asked me. "Would you agree to anything I say, Yui-en?"

"Of course, I will," I replied.

"Are you sure that you won't disobey me?," he repeated, and when I again agreed, he continued, "Go, then, and kill a thousand people and your birth in the Pure Land is settled."

"Even though that is your order," I protested, "and even with the capacity for evil within me, I cannot kill even a single person."

"Then why did you just say that you would not disobey what I, Shinran, said?" And then he went on, "By this we know that if we could act according to our thoughts, we could kill a thousand people for the sake of birth in the Pure Land if so required. We do not kill, not because our thoughts are good but because we do not have the karma to kill even a single person. Yet, even though we do not want to injure anyone, we may

Not justify-ing
evil

be led to kill a hundred or a thousand people."

The gist of this statement is that when we think good thoughts, we think we are good; and when we think evil thoughts, we think we are evil, not realizing fully that it is not these thoughts but the inconceivable power of the Vow that makes our salvation possible.

Once there was a man who fell into wrong views proclaiming that he would intentionally do evil as a way of attaining birth, since the Vow is directed to those who are evil. Thus saying, he committed many evil deeds. When Shinran heard about this, he admonished in a letter, "Do not take poison just because there is an antidote." He made this point to correct such erroneous views, but not at all to say that evil is an obstacle to attaining birth.

Shinran, moreover, said, "If upholding the precepts and maintaining the disciplines are required for true entrusting, how could we ever hope to go beyond birth-and-death? It is only by encountering the Primal Vow that such hopeless beings like ourselves are shown to be prideful and haughty. And yet evil cannot be committed unless it is already within us."

Again, he said, "People who make a living by casting nets or fishing in the seas and rivers, those who sustain themselves by hunting wild life and catching birds in the moors and mountains, and people who pass their lives by trading and cultivating fields are all alike." According to Shinran, "Under the influence of our karmic past we human beings will do anything."

And yet, in recent years people put on the guise of striving on the nembutsu path. They claim that only good people should say the nembutsu. Or they post restrictions at gathering places, proclaiming that those who commit certain acts are prohibited from entering. Are these not the sort of people who show outwardly how wise, virtuous, and diligent they are, while inwardly cherishing vanity and falsehood?

Karmic evil committed because of taking pride in the Vow is also an effect of past karma. Thus, leave everything good and evil to the working of karma and single-heartedly entrust yourself to the Primal Vow. Such is the way of Other Power. In *Essentials of Faith Alone* it is said, "To what extent does one know the power of Amida's compassion when a person believes that salvation is impossible because of karmic evil?" For the very reason that we are guilty of taking pride in the Primal Vow, the true entrusting as the gift of Other Power is settled.

We can be free of taking pride in the Primal Vow only after we entrust ourselves to the Primal Vow, having extinguished karmic evil and blind passion. But if blind passion were extinguished, one is already a buddha; and for a buddha the Vow realized through five kalpas of profound thought would be useless.

Since the people who censure others for taking pride in the Primal Vow themselves are filled with blind passion and impurities, aren't they also guilty of taking pride in the Primal Vow? If so, what is the evil that takes pride in the Primal Vow and what is the evil that does not take pride in the Primal Vow? Indeed, all this debate reveals shallowness and immaturity.

once you've entrusted yourself to amitabha, the Bodhisattva extinguishes bad karma, thus evil actions/passions

XIV

Some people say that one should believe that heavy evils of eight billion kalpas can be extinguished in the single utterance of nembutsu. This view refers to an evil person, guilty of ten vices and five transgressions, who has never said the nembutsu throughout life but who for the first time at the moment of death is told by a good teacher: nembutsu uttered once shall extinguish the evils accumulated in eight billion kalpas, and nembutsu uttered ten times shall extinguish the evils accumulated in eighty billion kalpas, thus leading to birth in the Pure Land. Is the single utterance or ten utterances meant to suggest the relative weights of ten vices and five transgressions? If so, this refers to the utility value of nembutsu in extinguishing evil. This is far different from our understanding. The reason is that in the awakening of one thought-moment, having been illuminated by Amida's light, we are endowed with true entrusting which is firm as a diamond; thus, we are already included in the stage of the truly settled. When our life comes to an end, all the blind passions and evil hindrances are immediately transformed into the realization of the "wisdom of non-origination."

Realizing that without this compassionate Vow, wretched and evil beings such as ourselves can never go beyond birth-and-death, we should know that all the nembutsu said throughout our lifetime simply express our gratitude to the benevolence and virtues of Tathagata's compassion.

To believe that each saying of nembutsu extinguishes evil is to seek birth in the Pure Land by eliminating evil thoughts through one's own efforts. If that is the case, since every thought we think in life binds us to birth-and-death, we must say the nembutsu until the final moment, continuously and consistently, without ever attaining birth. But since karmic consequences are decisive, we may end our life because of unforeseen accidents or we may be tormented by illness without ever attaining right-mindedness. Saying the nembutsu in such a state would be, indeed, most difficult. How are we to extinguish evil in such a state? If evil cannot be extinguished, then is attaining birth impossible?

When we entrust ourselves to the Vow that grasps us never to abandon us, we shall quickly attain birth, regardless of whether we commit evils for unknown reasons and even end our lives without saying the nembutsu. And when we say the nembutsu spontaneously, our trust in Amida becomes stronger and our gratitude to Tathagata becomes deeper as we approach the moment of supreme enlightenment. To desire to extinguish evil is the thought of self-power, the intention of those who hope to achieve right-mindedness at the moment of death. This shows the lack of true entrusting which is made possible by the working of Other Power.

XV

Some people say that one can attain enlightenment in this very body filled with blind passion. This is completely out of the question.

The doctrine of attaining Buddhahood in this very body is the essential teaching of Shingon Esoterism, the ultimate attainment of the three esoteric practices. And the purifying of the six sense-organs is the doctrine of the One Vehicle teaching of the *Lotus Sutra,* the attainment of the four blissful practices. These are all difficult practices performed by superior religious adepts and enlightenment realized through perfecting meditative practices. In contrast, the enlightenment that unfolds in the next birth is the essence of the Pure Land way of Other Power, the true entrusting which is settled and final. This is the effortless practice undertaken by inferior religious practicers in which the distinction between good and evil is non-existent.

Since it is unthinkably difficult to sunder blind passion and evil hindrances in this present life, the virtuous monks of Shingon and Tendai disciplinary practices also pray for enlightenment in the life to come. How much more so for ordinary people like ourselves! Although the upholding of precepts and attainment of wisdom are lacking, when we have crossed the painful ocean of birth-and-death on the vessel of Amida's Vow, reaching the Other Shore of the land of Fulfillment, the dark clouds of blind passion immediately vanish and the moon of enlightenment, dharma-as-it-is, appears instantaneously. Having become united with the Unhindered Light that illuminates the ten quarters, we bring benefits to all beings. This is true enlightenment.

Do those who believe in attaining enlightenment in

this very body reveal themselves in various forms of enlightenment, as did the historical Sakyamuni? Do they possess the thirty-two features and eighty characteristics of an enlightened being? Do they benefit sentient beings by expounding the Buddha Dharma? This is what constitutes enlightenment in this life. Shinran writes:

When true entrusting, firm as a diamond,
Is settled, at that very instant
Amida'a light grasps us and protects us,
And we forever transcend birth-and-death.

This means that when true entrusting is realized, Amida grasps us never to abandon us, and we no longer transmigrate through the six realms. When we understand this fully, how can we confuse it with the enlightenment in this life? How sad that such a misunderstanding exists. As the late master said, "In the true teaching of Pure Land I have been taught that in this life we entrust ourselves to the Primal Vow and in the Pure Land attain supreme enlightenment."

XVI

Some people say that if a practicer of true entrusting should unexpectedly become angry, act wantonly, or argue with others, they should by all means undergo turning-of-mind. Does this mean that we should sunder evil and practice good?

In the person of single-hearted nembutsu the turning-of-mind occurs only once. The turning-of-mind refers to this: transformation of those ignorant of the Primal Vow of Other Power who, being granted Amida's wisdom and realizing the impossibility of everyday mind attaining birth, abandon the old mind and entrust the self to the Primal Vow.

If it is necessary to undergo the turning-of-mind, day and night, about every deed in order to attain birth, we may die before doing so, or before nurturing tenderness and forbearance, since our lives may come to an end between the inhaling and exhaling of breath. Then the Primal Vow which grasps us never to abandon us would have no meaning.

Even though some may claim to entrust themselves to the Primal Vow, they actually feel that only the good are saved, no matter how great the inconceivable power of the Vow to save evil doers. To that extent they are doubting the power of the Vow, lacking the thought of entrusting themselves to the Vow, and will be born in the borderland. How lamentable this is!

Once true entrusting is settled, we realize that our birth is due to the working of Amida and not to our calculations. Even though we may do evil, even more should we think about the power of the Vow. Then, tenderness and forbearance will appear by virtue of "made to become so by itself."

In all matters regarding birth it is not necessary to contrive or design but always remember and become absorbed in the deep and profound compassion of Amida. Then we shall be able to say the nembutsu spontaneously, "made to become so by itself." When I do not contrive or calculate, I am "made to become so by itself." This is none other than the working of Other Power. And yet to my regret I hear some people talking knowingly about being "made to become so by itself" as if it were something special. How deplorable this is!

XVII

Some people say that those born in the borderland will eventually fall into hell. What attesting passage makes this claim?

This is asserted by those who claim to be scholars, and that is truly deplorable. How are they reading the sutras, commentaries, and teachings? I have been taught that people who lack true entrusting, doubting the Primal Vow, are born in the borderland, where they atone for evil karma and ultimately attain enlightenment in the land of Fulfillment.

Since true entrusting is very rare, many people go to the temporary land. And yet to contend that they are ultimately hopeless is to accuse the Buddha of falsehood.

XVIII

Some people say that the amount of offerings made to the Buddha Dharma will determine the size, great or small, that we will become as buddhas.

First of all, is it possible to determine the size of buddha, whether great or small? Even though the size of Buddha in the Pure Land is described in the sutra, it is the manifestation of dharmakaya-as-compassion, appearing for the sake of human beings. When one attains supreme enlightenment and realizes dharmakaya-as-it-is, how can size be discussed, since such shapes as long or short, square or round, do not exist; and color is also transcended, whether it be blue, yellow, red, white, or black?

Some say that they see the transformed Buddha when uttering the nembutsu. Could they have based their view on such statements as the following and applied it here, "In loud utterance one sees a huge Buddha and in quiet utterance one sees a small Buddha"?

Furthermore, although offerings can be part of the practice of selfless giving, no matter how many valuables we present to the Buddha or give to our teachers, the act is meaningless if true entrusting is absent. If one is made to give the self up to Other Power and true entrusting is complete, even though one does not present even a single sheet of paper or even half a coin to the Buddha Dharma, he or she is in accord with the intention of the Primal Vow.

Are people intimidating their fellow practicers, using the teaching as a pretext, to fulfill their own selfish needs?

EPILOGUE

I feel that the preceding views all arise due to differences in the understanding of true entrusting. According to our late master Shinran, it was the same at the time of his teacher, Honen. Among his disciples, there were only a few people who truly entrusted themselves to Amida. This was once a cause of debate between Shinran and fellow disciples. When he claimed, "Shinran's entrusting and Honen's entrusting are identical," Seikan, Nenbutsu, and others strongly refuted this, saying,

"How can you claim that our master's entrusting and your entrusting are identical!" To this Shinran replied, "Our master's wisdom and knowledge are truly profound and to say that our entrusting to Amida are identical is preposterous. But as far as true entrusting, leading to birth in the Pure Land is concerned, no difference exists at all. Both are the same." Still they continued to press Shinran, challenging him by saying, "How can that be possible?"

They finally decided to settle the argument once and for all by going to Honen, relating the details. When Honen listened to their respective views, he said, "The true entrusting of Honen is a gift granted by the Tathagata, and the true entrusting of Shinran is also a gift from the Tathagata. Thus, they are the same. People whose entrusting is different will probably not go to the same Pure Land as I."

Such was the case in earlier times, and today it seems that among the followers of single-hearted nembutsu there are some who do not share the same entrusting as that of Shinran. Although I may sound repetitious, I want to put all this down in writing.

Since my life, like a dew drop, still hangs onto this body which may be likened to withered grass, I am able to hear the doubts of my fellow practicers and tell them what I have learned from my teacher. But I fear and lament that after my eyes close and life comes to an end, there may arise chaos because of divergent interpretations.

When you are confused by different views, such as the above, you should carefully read the scriptures approved and used by our late master. Among scriptures generally you will find a mixture of teachings which are true and real and which are accommodating and tentative. The master's basic instruction was for us to choose the real, abandoning those accommodating the desires of the people, and select the real, rejecting the tentatively presented. Be very careful to see such differences among the scriptures. I have listed a few statements that attest to true entrusting, including them here for easy reference.

The master constantly said, "When I ponder on the compassionate Vow of Amida, established through five kalpas of profound thought, it was for myself, Shinran, alone. Because I am a being burdened so heavily with karma, I feel even more deeply grateful to the Primal Vow which is made to decisively save me."

As I now reflect upon these words, they are no different from the saying of Shan-tao: "Truly know that this self is a foolish being of karmic evil, repeating birth-and-death since beginningless aeons ago, forever drowning and wandering without ever knowing the path of liberation." How grateful I am that Shinran expressed this in his own person to make us deeply realize that we do not know the depth of karmic evil and that we do not know the height of Tathagata's benevolence, both of which cause us to live in utter confusion.

In reality, all of us, including myself, talk only about what is good and evil without thinking of the Tathagata's compassion. Our master once said, "I do not know what the two, good and evil, really mean. I could say that I know what good is, if I knew good as thoroughly and completely as the Tathagata. And I could say I know what evil is, if I knew evil as thoroughly and completely as the Tathagata. But in this impermanent world, like a burning house, all things are empty and vain, therefore, untrue. Only the nembutsu is true, real, and sincere.

Among the lies we say to each other, one is truly to be lamented. This occurs when some people who, in talking about the nembutsu, discuss true entrusting among themselves or try to explain it to others, and in order to silence people or stop further inquiry they even ascribe words to Shinran which were never spoken by him. How deplorable and regrettable this is! You should carefully think about this and reflect on it.

Although the above are not all my own words, they may at times sound a bit strange, because I am not too well versed in the sutras and commentaries. Also, I have yet to clearly perceive the depth of the teaching. But I have tried my best to recall some fragments, perhaps one one-hundredth, of what the late Shinran taught and have put them down in writing. How sad it is, if those who are fortunate enough to say the nembutsu are not immediately born in the land of Fulfillment but must continue residing in the borderland.

In tears I have dipped my brush in ink and have written this in the hope that conflicting views of true entrusting will not prevail among fellow practicers of nembutsu gathered together in a single room. Thus, I have called this *Tannisho: Lamenting the Deviations*. It should not be shown to outsiders.

AFTERWORD

HOW TO READ THE *TANNISHO*

The teaching of Shinran, transmitted as Jodo Shinshu (known as Shin Buddhism in the West), brings the depth of the Buddha Dharma to people in simple, clear language. Appearing from the heart of true compassion, it responds to the spiritual needs of everyone — not only the privileged, select few who can afford the time and resources to pursue religious practices, either full-time or part-time. As the working of great compassion, it assures everyone the liberation from the darkness of ignorance and the attainment of supreme enlightenment.

But this fact can be truly appreciated only in so far as one goes beyond the objective and rational approach. The objective approach seeks an answer based upon the subject-object framework. Such questions as "What is Shin Buddhism?" or "What is Amida Buddha?" separates the subject, the questioner, from any meaningful answer that may be forthcoming. The teaching remains unrelated to one's burning questions and deepest concerns. Consequently, the Buddha Dharma has no vital relevance to one's everyday life. The rational approach is based on a purely intellectual comprehension which excludes or suppresses the needs of the heart; the unconscious, instinctual and somatic self is completely disregarded. Since the Buddha Dharma addresses the whole person, it satisfies the deepest intellectual, emotional and volitional needs of the total self.

In the experience of Shinran the Buddha Dharma is realized intimately as the Buddha of Immeasurable Light and Immeasurable Life, the Buddha Amida. Thus,

Amida is referred to in endearing terms, such as *Oya-sama*, meaning my dear father, my dear mother. Immeasurable Light illuminates the fundamental human condition and awakens us to our limited, imperfect and mortal selves. It shows us why our life is characterized by insecurity and disrupted by greed, anger and folly. When this is felt deeply, we have already been touched by the Light of true compassion; the working of Light, warm and compassionate, proceeds to transform existential unease into profound gratitude for this life. This working is simultaneous with that of Immeasurable Life that pervades all beings, awakening each of us to ultimate reality here and now, not in some uncertain future. Our limited life-unto-death is but another manifestation of Immeasurable Life that has no beginning and no end. Immeasurable Light and Immeasurable Life enable us to become our truly human selves.

This truth is brought to vivid reality in the saying of nembutsu — "Namu-amida-butsu" — which is the deep wish, called the Primal Vow of Amida, touching each of us, so that we may be liberated from self-delusion. The saying of nembutsu affirms that this limited self, "namu" — imperfect, fallible and mortal self — is sustained by "amida-butsu," unlimited, boundless Light and Life. The nembutsu, "Namu-amida-butsu," as an unified experience, coming from the depth of life itself, grasps us and transforms us, enabling us to awaken to ultimate reality. Here it must be realized that in Buddhist understanding neither the "self" nor the "Buddha" is a fixed, static object; rather, each is a fluid aspect of dynamic reality that is constantly becoming. Because nothing is fixed or final, the limited, imperfect self, just as it is, can be transformed into a being of supreme enlightenment. Such is the wonder of Buddhism.

This dynamic process, made real and concrete by

the nembutsu, works in different ways at various junctures in one's life. Awakening to Namu-amida-butsu solves difficulties in human relationships, ameliorates hardships and sufferings, provides wise counsel when confronted with difficult choices, inspires timely and compassionate action, transforms sorrow into joy, and gives us the power to see and criticize false social constructs. Living the nembutsu with full awareness of human limitedness leads us not to denigrate but to celebrate life within the boundless wisdom and compassion of Amida Buddha.

Such in brief is Shinran's basic teaching, a rich tapestry woven from so-called Pure Land scriptures and original insights developed within Mahayana Buddhism, which arose in the first century B.C.E. in India. Later transmitted to the vast reaches of the Asian continent, today it is now touching the shores of the Western world. Among the array of Mahayana scriptures, three classic texts were selected as foundational to the Pure Land tradition: *Larger Sutra of Immeasurable Life (Daimuryoju-kyo), Smaller Sutra of Immeasurable Life (Amida-kyo)*, and *Meditation Sutra (Kanmuryoju-kyo)*.

Among them, the most important is the Larger Sutra which reveals the mythic history of Amida Buddha fulfilling 48 major vows, all designed to meet the specific needs of people — psychological, emotional, physical and spiritual (mythic here refers to that which is true and real beyond ordinary understanding). Among them the crucial one is the 18th Vow which culminates in the forging of the nembutsu as the ultimate gift to humankind. It is a priceless gift, for anyone who is touched by it becomes transformed and achieves supreme enlightenment. The nembutsu enables us to lead a natural, spontaneous life in direct contrast to our normal life, filled with self-centered calculations and anxieties. The light of true compassion reveals them for what they are, nullifying their negative consequences. But an immense struggle is involved in realizing the spontaneous life of nembutsu, a struggle which some of us may undergo as the "transformation through the three vows." As conceived by Shinran, it refers to the progressive levels of religious life contained in the 19th, 20th, and 18th vows.

As mature human beings, we all aspire to the ethical life. The stage of the 19th vow encourages good conduct, moral rectitude, religious piety and adherence to scripture. But when one is made to realize that even the highest good may be tainted by egoistic concerns and that religious piety may simply be self-serving, one is ready to move into the world of the 20th vow. Here reliance on self-generated power is abandoned, and one embraces the sole practice of nembutsu as the working of Other Power. All other religious disciplines, such as observing monastic vows, meditative endeavors, and various religious rituals, are regarded as superfluous. Recitative nembutsu alone is considered to be meaningful and productive. But even such a practice can unconsciously fall into the trap of merit accumulation based on self-power. It then becomes another form of ego-assertion that obstructs the working of Other Power. As a result, a person is subject to unease and anxiety.

The true nembutsu comes to life in the 18th vow, when unlimited life realizes itself in a person, and that person embodies the universe of the 18th vow. That is, a limited being becomes liberated from entrapment in self-delusion and manifests life that is most natural and spontaneous. Although the passage from the 20th vow to the 18th vow is closed to the designs of self-power, the compassion of the Buddha reaches down into the world of the 20th vow to touch all beings. The Primal Vow, thus, affirms the limited self as inseparable from unlimited life at every moment of life; and when our karmic life becomes exhausted, we become one with boundless life in all its richness and manifestations.

In sum, the transformation through the ethical stage (19th vow) to the self-generated religious stage (20th vow) and finally to the truly accomplished stage (18th vow) shows the evolution of spirituality which continues as an ever deepening awareness of the finite (human beings) sustained by the infinite (Amida Buddha). At the core of this transformation is the penetrating insight into the delusions of the ego-self, born from the unfathomable darkness of ignorance, and brought to full realization through the working of the Primal Vow. The focus is on the unlimited and boundless compassion of Amida Buddha — not the deluded self — which touches every phase of human life. Having described the essentials of Shinran's teaching, we now turn to highlight its significant features which make it a unique expression of the Buddha Dharma.

The primary question for Shinran is the efficacy of religious practice. It is easy to pursue practices of various kinds, but rare is it to obtain the desired results. None of the existing paths that Shinran attempted led to ultimate fulfillment. He recognized the bankruptcy of practice both within himself and without in monastic institutions. In his words, "The Primal Vow is established for those of us who cannot become freed from the bondage of birth-and-death through any religious practice, due to the abundance of blind passion" *(Tannisho III)*. Two points require elaboration in this admission: first, the radical rejection of existing forms of religious practice, based on twenty years of dedicated disciplines in the Tendai Buddhist tradition; and second, the admission of massive blind passion which could not be overcome through any existing religious practice.

The first realization in Shinran's case was

compounded by the socio-historical sense of *mappo*, that the end-time of history spelled the doom of institutional Buddhism and everything connected with it. For him religious practice was a matter of life and death, a matter of total commitment to the monastic life, including renunciation of all family ties, adherence to strict precepts, including celibacy, and the goal was nothing less than buddhahood. In spite of his conscientious dedication, however, the practices he pursued did not produce any fruitful result, and institutional Buddhism could not provide any support, for the whole world itself was disintegrating and collapsing.

The bankruptcy of practice led to the second, much more powerful, realization: the depth of blind passion which permeates every human thought, speech and action, all testifying to the undeniable fact of human limitedness. According to Buddhist reflection, passion is an instinctual, emotive force arising from the unconscious and deeply rooted in the body. When it becomes intertwined with egocentric human calculations, it becomes distorted and causes havoc in our lives. Thus, as long as human existence means having a body, a person is forever bound to all kinds of limitations and bondages. This is the infinite finitude of samsara.

Since traditional forms of religious practice, such as meditative or contemplative disciplines, normally fail to reach the deep core of blind passion, Shinran focused on the practice of *monpo*, "deep hearing of the Dharma." Deep hearing leads to a twofold awakening: appreciating the boundless compassion of Amida, and simultaneously seeing into the bottomless depth of blind passion. The compiler of the *Tannisho* went even further when he acknowledged the lack of thoroughgoing penetration into both kinds of awareness:

How grateful I am that Shinran expressed this in his own person to make us deeply realize that we do not know the depth of karmic evil and that we do not know the height of Tathagata's benevolence, both of which cause us to live in utter confusion (Epilogue).

Deep hearing, then, is not just an auditory sensation, involving the ear, but a matter of the whole person. "Deep hearing of the Dharma" means embodying the Buddha Dharma, an experiential awakening of the total self, conscious and unconscious, mind and body.

A synonym of hearing the Dharma, *monpo,* is an unusual expression, *monko,* or "hearing the Light." This phrase suggests that authentic hearing brings to light the hidden karmic self of blind passion rooted in the body. This is the reason that Daiei Kaneko, a leading spokesman of contemporary Shin Buddhism, urges, "Receive material gifts with your heart and receive the Buddha Dharma with your body." It is with this body that the Buddha Dharma is truly realized.

Deep hearing, synonymous with true awakening, is made possible by the working of the Buddha or Tathagata. According to Shinran, "The Tathagata is Light. Light is none other than wisdom; wisdom takes the form of light. But wisdom is, in fact, formless; therefore, this Tathagata is the Buddha of inconceivable light. This Tathagata fills the countless worlds in the ten quarters, and so is called the Buddha of Boundless Light" (*Notes on Once-calling* and *Many-calling,* p. 46). When a person is thus touched by Light, an awareness beyond conceptual understanding occurs; Shinran calls it the wisdom that is drawn out of the foolish being by the power of true compassion. In his formulation,

A sutra states that Avalokitesvara...reveals itself as the deity of the sun and dispels the darkness of ignorance in all beings; and Mahasthamaprapta... appears as the deity of the moon and illuminates the long night of birth-and-death. Together they bring forth wisdom in all beings (*Notes on the Essentials of Faith Alone*, pp. 31-32).

The symbolism of Light reveals not only the working of wisdom but also of compassion. In the Buddhist tradition compassion is all-embracing, non-judgmental, warm and nurturing. All-embracing compassion means that everyone is saved equally, but special concern and love are shown to those who recognize their weakness, powerlessness and foolishness as limited beings. As such, it is not judgmental, for no one is regarded as dispensable and everyone receives nurturing for supreme enlightenment. Even the lowliest in the eyes of society can attain the highest awakening, due to the transformation wrought by true compassion. The warmth of compassion melts evil to transform it into good, making possible the flowering of each person's fullest potential. This process is known as *jinen*, "made to become so by itself and for itself." As explained by Shinran,

"To be made to become so" means that without the practicer's calculation in any way whatsoever, all the past, present, and future evil karma are transformed into the highest good. To be transformed means that evil karma, without being nullified or eradicated, is made into the highest good, just as all river waters, upon entering the great ocean, immediately become ocean water (*Notes*, pp. 32-33).

An even more graphic metaphor for transformation states: "When we entrust ourselves to the Tathagata's

Primal Vow, we who are like bits of tiles and pebbles are transmuted into gold" (*Notes*, pp. 40-41). Historically speaking, at the time of Shinran those "who are like bits of tiles and pebbles" included the disenfranchised in medieval Japan: people who violated life to make a living, hunters, fisherfolk, peasants, and so on; those who preyed on others, such as peddlers and merchants; monks and nuns who had violated the precepts; and women of all classes. Shinran identifies with such people considered as "bad" in the eyes of privileged society and excluded from entering the Buddhist path. The compassion of Buddha, however, all the more focuses on such abandoned people and eventually "transmutes them into gold," into human beings of true and real worth.

Such an understanding forms the basis of the paradoxical claim by Shinran that "Even the good person is saved, how much more so the evil doer" *(Tannisho III)*. This should not be read as a negation of ethical life, or as a license to do evil, but as a penetrating recognition of human reality at its depth — limited, imperfect and mortal — yet sustained and protected by Immeasurable Light and Immeasurable Life. This simultaneous appreciation — finite existence and infinite reality, related to each other in double exposure — is traditionally expressed in the phrase, *ki-ho ittai* — the unity *(ittai)* of the limited, finite self *(ki)* and unlimited dharmic reality *(ho)*.

In everyday life whenever we experience our human limitation in outbursts of anger, jealousy, hatred, lust and fear, it is the Buddha Dharma that reveals their true reality to us, making them transparent and showing us the unlimited life that flows below them. When this experience is verbalized, the spontaneous saying of Namu-amida-butsu occurs. The awakening to the limited self *(namu)* is made possible by the working of unlimited life and light *(amida-butsu)*. Shinran expresses this in a deeply personal way: "When I ponder on the Primal Vow of Amida, established through five kalpas of profound thought, I realize that it is for myself, Shinran, alone" (*Tannisho* Epilogue). Here Shinran is not speaking as an unreflecting, egocentric being but is affirming the single one, irreplaceable and unique, who lives interrelated and interconnected with all beings. As such, each self is affirmed as manifesting ultimate significance and worth.

The nembutsu is the Sacred Name *(myogo)*, the source of spirituality and focus of devotional life. The central image in Shin Buddhist worship is not the image of the historical Buddha, nor the sculpted or painted figure of Amida Buddha; rather, it is "Namu-amida-butsu." Fundamentally, the Sacred Name is the self-articulation of basic reality, expressing itself in language that makes it accessible to anyone who has the ability to hear deeply. Since the Sacred Name is neither a concept to be understood nor a proposition to be figured out, anyone, at anytime, under any circumstance can call on the Name.

In living "Namu-amida-butsu" there is no dogma to uphold, no religious authority to follow, and no special teacher or guru to revere. It is in this spirit that Shinran, who, in spite of having hundreds of known followers, proclaimed, "As for myself, Shinran, I do not have a single disciple" *(Tannisho VI)*. Behind this disclaimer is also the affirmation of the interconnectedness of all life as expressed in his proclamation: "All beings have been mothers and fathers, sisters and brothers in the timeless process of birth-and-death" *(Tannisho V)*. He calls all those who walk the path of Buddha Dharma, "fellow seekers, fellow practicers."

This interconnectedness with life, however, extends not only to humans but to all beings, both animate and inanimate. Based upon the central

Mahayana philosophy of interdependence and interpenetration, Shinran writes:

> The Tathagata pervades the countless worlds; it fills the hearts and minds of the ocean of all beings. Thus, plants, trees, and land all attain Buddhahood. Since it is with this heart and mind of all sentient beings that they entrust themselves to the Vow of Dharmakaya-as-compassion (Amida Buddha), this entrusting is none other than Buddha-nature (*Notes*, p. 42).

The Tathagata or Buddha as fundamental reality pervades everything in countless worlds, providing the source of life and creativity. This source fuels the energy in nature, so that plants, trees and land fully realize their potentials. The same source enables human beings to become liberated from their ego-self by virtue of Immeasurable Life and Light and thus become truly human. This is none other than Buddha-nature actualized in a person and attaining its fullest flowering.

We now turn to discussing some key terms to further our understanding of Shin Buddhism, including self-power and Other Power, true entrusting, good and evil, nembutsu, and birth in the Pure Land.

SELF-POWER AND OTHER POWER

The terms, self-power and Other Power, are central to understanding the Shin Buddhist experience. First used by the Chinese master T'an-luan (476-542), they became crucial in the teaching of Honen and Shinran. According to the latter, self-power refers to a person who is always "conscious of doing good" *(Tannisho III)*, whether that "good" be in terms of moral deeds or religious pieties. Such a good is rooted in unconscious ego-centeredness; this is self-power that defiles every thought, action and speech with self-interest. Manifested in willful calculations and contrivances, it plunges a person ever more deeply into the quagmire of samsara.

Other Power is defined by Shinran as "that which is devoid of self-centered calculations." In that sense it is the opposite of self-power, yet the two are not absolutely disjunct, for Other Power is none other than great compassion, embracing self-power as an essential part of itself. When Other Power is seen opposed to self-power, that is an objectified, conceptualized view that has no relevance to Shin Buddhist life. Thus, Saichi, the unlettered Shin devotee, wrote,

> There is no self-power
> No other power
> All is Other Power.

The person who is driven by self-power on the path of enlightenment inevitably fails because of its self-serving nature, yet very few of us are free of self-power. This is clearly recognized by Shinran when he describes himself as a person "who cannot become freed from the bondage of birth-and-death through any religious

practice, due to the abundance of blind passion"
(Tannisho III). The major obstacle on the Buddhist path
is not the difficulty of practice, lack of good teachers, or
inadequate support systems, but self-power or blind
passion *(bonno)* that lies hidden within our unconscious.
Blind passion erupts in greed, anger and folly; it is the
source of hatred, jealousy and violence; it gives rise to
arrogance, hypocrisy and self-hate. But such a person,
called a "foolish being" *(bombu)*, is the primary concern
of Amida's compassion. Shinran made this point clearly
in *Tannisho IX:*

> The working of blind passion also causes us
> not to want to go to the Pure Land and makes
> us feel uneasy, worrying about death when
> we become even slightly ill. Impossible it
> seems to leave this old house of agitation
> where we have wandered aimlessly since the
> beginning of time...This is due to blind
> passion, so truly powerful and overwhelming.
> But no matter how reluctant we may be, when
> our life in this world comes to an end, beyond
> our control, then for the first time we go to the
> land of Fulfillment. Those who do not want to
> go immediately are the special concern of true
> compassion.

Other Power is not an absolute being, a miracle
worker, or something separate from ourselves. Rather, it
is dynamic life, open and boundless, realizing itself in a
foolish being. In so doing, the being of self-power and
blind passion is transformed into its very opposite,
liberated, free and authentic. In the words of Shinran,
"When I do not contrive, it is called 'made to become so
by itself.' This is none other than Other Power"
(Tannisho XVI). The Japanese original for "made to
become so by itself" is *jinen* which is composed of two
parts: *ji* or "self" and *nen* which means "made to
become so." In other words, each *ji*, whether a person, a

flower, a tree, a mountain, or any other phenomenal particular, each possessing its own unique selfhood, realizes its fullest potential completely. In the same way the Primal Vow of Amida works on each foolish being, liberating one from a fictive self to become authentic in the fullest sense. Shoji Hamada, an eminent Japanese potter, felt this sense of Other Power, when he wrote:

> If a kiln is small, I might be able to control it completely, that is to say, my own self can become a controller, a master of the kiln. But man's own self is but a small thing after all. When I work at the large kiln, the power of my own self becomes so feeble that it cannot control it adequately. It means that for the large kiln, the power that is beyond me is necessary. Without the mercy of such an invisible power I cannot get good pieces. One of the reasons why I wanted to have a large kiln is because I want to be a potter, if I may, who works more in grace than in his own power. You know nearly all the best old pots were done in huge kilns (Soetsu Yanagi, *The Unknown Craftsman*, p. 224).

This working of Other Power is praised, above all, as great compassion by one who comes to realize the limited, imperfect and mortal self, for it converts the lowest into the highest, evil into good. This is what Shinran meant when he says, "bits of tiles and pebbles are transmuted into gold." The inner dynamic of this transmutation or transformation is contained in the following assertion: "Evil karma, without being nullified or eradicated, is made into the highest good, just as all river waters, upon entering the great ocean, immediately become ocean water."

The radical transformation, made real by the Primal Vow of Amida, occurs throughout the life of the foolish person, inevitably and necessarily culminating

in supreme enlightenment. This process at the core of
Shin life is called *shinjin,* rendered as "true entrusting"
or "pure faith." In both cases "true" and "pure" denote
the Buddha's compassionate activity within us which
insures our entrusting or our faith. Thus, *shinjin* may
also be rendered as "endowed trust," because it is a gift
from Other Power. At any rate, this central experience
of *shinjin* is not a matter of attitude, belief or conviction
but of being awakened to unlimited, immeasurable life
that sustains our limited human existence. What this
involves will be discussed under true entrusting.

TRUE ENTRUSTING

The purpose of human life is accomplished when we experience true entrusting, whereby a limited, foolish being realizes its unity with unlimited Other Power (referred to earlier as *ki-ho ittai*). This unity is not a collapsing into undifferentiated oneness, for the distinction between a foolish being and Amida Buddha remains as long as we are human beings. It is a non-dual relationship in which a foolish being remains forever a foolish being until the moment of death, when one is liberated from all karmic bondage. Yet at each moment of samsaric life the compassionate working of Other Power never ceases to perform its miraculous work of transformation. The basic framework of this non-dual relationship was given its classical formulation by Shan-tao (613 – 681):

> Profound mind is the mind of profound awakening. There are two aspects. First, to decisively and deeply awaken to this self at this very moment as a mortal of birth-and-death, resulting from past karmic evil, who has been drowning and repeating the cycle of birth-and-death from timeless past to this very present with no hope of ever achieving emancipation. Second, to decisively and deeply awaken to the forty-eight com-passionate vows of Amida Buddha which embrace sentient beings and without fail make them attain birth in the Pure Land by carrying them on the power of the vows without any hesitation or question whatsoever (*The True Teaching, Practice, and Realization of the Pure Land Way*, Volume II, p. 213).

True entrusting, thus, grows from a dynamic, creative tension between two forces: unlimited compassion and limited samsaric existence. And it moves in two opposing directions which become ultimately one and the same: 1) entrusting the self to one's own limited, karmic existence, and 2) simultaneously entrusting oneself to unlimited and boundless compassion of Amida Buddha. Together they form *ki-ho-ittai*.

True entrusting, thus, means awakening to the reality of oneself and of Other Power. A great lay teacher of nembutsu, Eikichi Ikeyama, clarified this in verse:

> The Pure I, which is not I,
> Being in me, reveals to me
> This defiled I.

The "Pure I" is Other Power, Amida Buddha, the unlimited dimension of self. Although it may remain obscure to most of us, yet it is always with us. Sooner or later in life, however, it will reveal itself and illuminate the other aspect of ourselves, the "defiled I." This is the limited, karmic self of foolish being — our true reality — which remains unknown to us until illuminated by the Pure I. Both are essential aspects of ourselves that are brought to simultaneous awareness by true compassion. No amount of psychological analysis, based on dichotomous thinking, can bring about such a radical realization to a person.

The two-fold structure of true entrusting is based on the fundamental philosophy of Mahayana Buddhism that affirms delusion as an essential part of enlightenment. That is, supreme enlightenment sees its opposite, delusion, as a essential component of itself, for it is the very reason for the compassionate working of transformation. This nondual relationship is expressed metaphorically by Shinran as follows:

Evil hindrance becomes the contents of virtue,
As in the case of ice and water.
The more the ice, the more the water;
The more the hindrance, the more the virtue.

Having realized true entrusting majestic
and boundless
By the working of Unhindered Light,
The ice of blind passion melts without fail
To instantly become the water of enlightenment.
(*Koso-wasan*, Verses 39 and 40)

Evil hindrance includes karmic evil, blind passion, darkness of ignorance; and virtue is a Buddhist synonym for enlightenment. The proper understanding of this relationship, however, is appreciated only by having a clear grasp of fundamental evil which underlies conventional notions of good and evil.

GOOD AND EVIL

One of the major themes in the *Tannisho* is the problem of good and evil. We must consider at least three basic kinds of good and evil: legal, moral and religious.

On the legal plane, good and evil, right and wrong, are determined objectively, based on a codified law which is applied to all people in all circumstances. The final judgment of good and evil depends on the concrete evidence presented.

On the moral plane, however, the determination of what is good and evil is frequently determined by the conscience and integrity of a person. It may not be easily evident to others; in fact, it can be completely beyond public scrutiny. For example, a person may not be legally guilty of any offense, yet one may feel bad about not having acted properly. It may be purely subjective, yet conscience is at the core of what it means to be an ethical human being.

Religiously speaking, good and evil are regarded from a radically different perspective. While on the ethical and moral plane, they are seen from a horizontal viewpoint, so to speak, on the religious plane they are seen from a vertical viewpoint. That is, good and evil are not situated objectively as a matter of preference or choice, for underlying both are the movements of the ego-self. Whether we choose good or evil in the ordinary sense, it is from a profoundly self-centered position. The noblest good may be self-serving; the avoidance of evil may be a matter of expedience. Since evil in this deeper sense has roots in the karmic past, it is called karmic evil.

Such an awareness of karmic evil is beyond rational comprehension, but it can be revealed to us by the illumination of the Primal Vow. Thus, the realization of karmic evil *(ki)* and the Primal Vow *(ho)* are simultaneous and inseparable. When the two are separately grasped, all kinds of distortions appear. The one-sided focus on karmic evil can easily become obsessive and destructive, even leading to the boasting and justifying of evil. Shinran foresaw this possibility among those of shallow understanding and issued his warning, "Do not take poison, just because there is an antidote" *(Tannisho XIII).* On the other hand, the exclusive reliance on Other Power, lacking awareness of karmic evil, can lead to self-inflation and triumphalism. Both arise from an unconscious attachment to a false, deluded self which obstructs true entrusting to Other Power. The tension that exists between the two aspects of entrusting is clarified by Saichi:

> When evil is not realized, the Buddha is
>   not realized.
> When evil is realized, the Buddha is realized.
> Evil and Buddha are one.
> This is Namu-amida-butsu in six syllables.
> How wretched, how wretched!
> How grateful, how grateful!

"Wretched" refers to the limited, imperfect being who cannot be liberated from self-delusion, insecurity and anxiety, no matter how sincerely religious practice is pursued. And "grateful" expresses profound appreciation to the working of the Primal Vow which assures complete liberation and identification with unlimited life, no matter who it may be.

The person of true entrusting now performs good and avoids evil in the conventional sense; they do so from a profound appreciation of having been affirmed as human beings in the religious sense. Shinran proclaims:

Amida's Primal Vow does not discriminate between the young and old, good and evil; true entrusting alone is essential. The reason is that the Vow is directed to the being burdened with the weight of karmic evil and burning with the flames of blind passion. Thus, in entrusting ourselves to the Primal Vow, no other form of good is necessary, for there is no good that surpasses the nembutsu. And evil need not be feared, for there is no evil which can obstruct the working of Amida's Primal Vow *(Tannisho I).*

NEMBUTSU

What does it mean to say that "there is no good that surpasses the nembutsu"? Before answering this basic question, some understanding of the different connotations of nembutsu may be helpful. Originally, the term meant "contemplation *(nen)* on the Buddha *(butsu)*"; later the term referred to "saying *(nen)* the name of the Buddha *(butsu)*" which provided a focus for meditative practice. Eventually the recitation was isolated from contemplative exercises to become the sole practice in Pure Land Buddhism.

This practice, however, is regarded not as a human activity but as the working of the Buddha manifested in a person. A popular Shin poem reads,

The nembutsu that flows
From this defiled mouth
Is the voice calling me
From countless kalpas past.

Thus, the saying of "Namu-amida-butsu" is called a mandate from the Buddha to give up the ego-self and entrust the self to Amida Buddha. One then becomes free of self-clinging and attunes oneself to the fundamental life pulsating throughout the universe. Since the initiative comes from Other Power, the nembutsu is understood as the self-articulation of fundamental reality, reaching us through the words, Namu-amida-butsu. When this is realized in a person, *shinjin* or true entrusting is born to become the primary cause leading to supreme enlightenment.

The nembutsu is truly meaningful only in so far as it has a personal impact, completely transforming one's life from negative to positive. When it is regarded objectively and treated as a mere concept, the nembutsu is trivialized. This trivialization is common among modern people who have separated mind from body and who deal with life merely from the cerebral standpoint. The nembutsu, however, does not recognize the mind-body division and deals with the instinctual needs of the body, the forces of blind passion, not to suppress them but to find channels for their creative expression. When this is fully realized, the nembutsu is experienced as the repository of accumulated Buddhist wisdom and compassion. The saying of nembutsu ultimately becomes the grand affirmation of life itself.

Since living the nembutsu transforms body and mind, conscious and unconscious, from the depth of blind passion, the foolish being attains liberation in the very midst of samsaric existence. This point was made precisely by Shinran when he said, "In the person of nembutsu opens up the great path of unobstructed freedom" *(Tannisho VII)*. This liberation and freedom from karmic bondage was expressed variously as entering the ocean of Amida's vow, transcending birth-and-death, being grasped never to be abandoned, joining the company of the truly settled, attaining the stage of nonretrogression, realizing *shinjin* of diamond-like firmness, and birth in the Pure Land.

Birth In the Pure Land

The traditional view of "birth in the Pure Land" was that a practicer would leave this defiled world and move forward on the path of enlightenment in the Pure Land after death. While it was not such a simple matter, nevertheless the goal of buddhahood was to be realized not in the here and now but in the future, because of the overwhelming obstacles to supreme enlightenment in this world. Shinran placed this in the context of Mahayana Buddhist philosophy and gave a radically new interpretation to the meaning of "birth in the Pure Land."

First, Shinran identified this phrase as another expression for attaining *shinjin,* the awakening to reality. While nonretrogression was descriptive of the highest stage reached by a bodhisattva on the path of supreme enlightenment, Shinran applied this to the nembutsu practicer of *shinjin* whose enlightenment is securely established in the Primal Vow of Amida. Thus, while remaining a person of blind passion, one attains "birth in the Pure Land" here and now and not in some distant future after death.

The famous saying, "in the preceding instant, life ends; in the subsequent instant, birth is attained," traditionally meant that when one dies, in the next moment one is born in the Pure Land. But Shinran interpreted this statement to mean that at the moment of *shinjin,* one's life of delusion ends and a new life of nembutsu begins, here and now. The emphasis is on the working of Other Power at every instant, transforming the unenlightened, foolish being into a being destined for supreme enlightenment. According to Shinran,

Then they attain birth means that when a person realizes *shinjin,* he or she is born immediately. To be born immediately means to dwell in the stage of nonretrogression. To dwell in the stage of nonretrogression is to become established in the stage of the truly settled. This is also called the attainment of the stage equal to enlightenment. Such is the meaning of *then they attain birth. Then* means immediately; immediately means without any passage of time, without any passage of days (*Notes on Essentials of Faith Alone,* pp. 34-35).

The phrase, "then they attain birth," comes from scripture normally understood as an event occurring after death in the Pure Land, but Shinran affirmed this as a crucial event, here and now, in this life.

The fact of supreme enlightenment, made real by the Primal Vow of Amida, also led him to describe the person of *shinjin* as identical with Maitreya Bodhisattva, awaiting the proper moment to appear as the next Buddha in this world. In Shinran's own words, "When sentient beings realize true entrusting, they attain the equal of perfect enlightenment, being of the same stage as Maitreya, the future Buddha. That is, they become established in the stage of the truly settled. Hence, true entrusting is like a diamond, never becoming crushed or fragmented; thus, Shinran speaks of 'diamond-like entrusting' " (*Notes,* p. 34).

While affirming that the person of nembutsu is the same as Maitreya, he also equates such a person to the Tathagata or Buddha. In both cases Shinran is clear and adamant that as long as human beings exist in their karmic manifestation, they remain forever as unenlightened, foolish beings, yet at the same time the working of true compassion enables people to transcend karmic bondages at every instant of this life.

Second, when our karmic life exhausts itself and we take leave of this world, the person of *shinjin* is born in the Pure Land to instantly attain supreme enlightenment. Having thus realized buddhahood, one immediately leaves the Pure Land and returns to the defiled world of samsara to work for the salvation of all beings. According to this understanding, the Pure Land is not a geographical place, a static ontological locale, but a symbol of supreme enlightenment, the source of wisdom and compassion. The going to the Pure Land and the returning from the Pure Land accords with the life of bodhisattva which is a never-ending movement of ascent to supreme enlightenment and simultaneous descent into samsara for the salvation of all beings. In this scheme samsara becomes the playground of salvific bodhisattva activity. This bodhisattva ideal is expressed thusly,

> Those who attain the Pure Land of peace
> Return to this evil world of five defilements,
> And like Sakyamuni Buddha
> Bring endless benefits to all beings.
> (*Jodo-wasan*, Verse 20)

That the Pure Land is symbolic of supreme enlightenment is made clear by Shinran, when he writes: "As to the true land, the *Larger Sutra* states: 'The Land of Immeasurable Light' and 'The realm of accumulated wisdom (of all Buddhas).' And the *Treatise on Pure Land* states: 'It is absolute, expansive, and limitless like space' " (*The True Teaching, Practice and Realization of the Pure Land Way*, Volume III, p. 439).

In the first quotation it must be clearly understood that there is no so-called "land" in the objective sense that emanates light; rather, wherever Immeasurable Light illuminates our human existence and liberates it from the binding forces of karmic evil, there is the dynamic Pure Land. And that the Pure Land is "absolute, expansive, and limitless like space" means that it is beyond our conceptual grasp which is relative, confining and limiting. Traditionally, the Pure Land is said to be inconceivable, indescribable and inexpressible, but this simply means that it is not an object of rational, discursive understanding. In fact, countless people have experienced the Pure Land here and now and at the moment of death, insuring the vitality of Shinran's transmission down through the centuries.

GLOSSARY

Amida Buddha — Literally, the Buddha of Immeasurable Life *(amitāyus,* symbolizing compassion) and Immeasurable Light *(amitābha,* symbolizing wisdom). Amida is not some kind of being but a dynamic salvific activity which leads a person to supreme enlightenment through Light, the radiance of true wisdom *(prajñā),* illuminating the darkest recesses of self and the world to transform negative karma into positive karma by the power of compassion *(karuṇā).*

Attesting Passage — Recorded sayings and passages from the writings of Shinran which attest to the truth of a given interpretation.

Birth (ōjō) — Abbreviation for "going to be born in the Pure Land" which is understood by Shinran in a twofold sense: 1) instantaneous awakening, here and now, occurs with *shinjin* or true entrusting; and 2) attaining of buddhahood at the moment of death when one sheds all karmic limitations and becomes one with Immeasurable Life and Light to begin the salvific work in samsara to liberate all beings.

Blind Passion (bonnō) — Deep-rooted and ineradicable self-centeredness contained in the unconscious which is one with the body, causing mental, emotional, and physical afflictions, which no amount of self-powered practice can overcome.

Borderland — Synonymous with such phrases as the castle of doubt, palace of womb, and realm of indolence, the person of self-power is born temporarily in the borderland before eventually attaining birth in the Pure Land.

Dharma — A key term in Buddhism which has two connotations: 1) reality as it is, synonymous with suchness, thusness, thingness, and so forth; and 2) the teaching expressing this reality, as in Buddha Dharma.

Dharmakāya-as-compassion — The body of reality manifested as compassion in order to help suffering beings transform negative karma into positive karma.

Distant Capital — Kyoto, the ancient capital of Japan, where Shinran spent the last decades of his life. His followers in Kanto, north of present-day Tokyo, travelled by foot to this faraway capital to receive guidance concerning questions regarding his teachings.

Effortless Practice — The nembutsu is effortless practice, since it is free of self-centered calculations. While no special effort, such as renunciation, celibacy, meditative practice, and so forth are required, an immense inner struggle occurs before achieving the life of spontaneity, naturalness and gratitude in the nembutsu.

Five Transgressions — Killing father, mother, monk, injuring the Buddha, and creating schisms in the Sangha (Hinayana Buddhism); vandalizing temples, statues, and scriptures, slandering the teaching, obstructing religious practices, violating the five precepts and committing ten evils (Mahayana Buddhism).

Foolish Being (bonbu) — Descriptive of human beings bound to aimless, samsaric life by radical ignorance and blind passion. Unable to attain deliverance by any religious practice, the foolish being all the more becomes the primary object of the Primal Vow.

Four Blissful Practices — Proper behavior in body, mind, and speech and the vow to lead all beings to freedom.

Four Modes of Birth — Life produced from the womb, from egg, from micro-organism, and from metamorphosis.

Grasped Never to be Abandoned — True compassion which affirms each person in a non-dichotomous relationship, such that there is no one who is forsaken or rejected.

Hōnen (1133-1212) — A revolutionary figure who founded an independent Pure Land (Jōdo) school in 1175 and was the teacher of Shinran, founder of Shin Buddhism.

Inconceivable (fushigi, fukashigi) — That which is beyond conceptual or rational understanding but brought to full awareness in a foolish being by the power of true compassion.

Karmic Evil — The fundamental human condition of fathomless ignorance which restricts our freedom; it is the primary object of the Primal Vow which reaches its depth and effects its transformation from the negative to positive.

Land of Fulfillment, True Fulfillment (hōdo) — The Pure Land of Amida Buddha, which was created by fulfilling the 48 vows. Also called the Land of Immeasurable Light, it symbolizes wisdom which illuminates the darkest recesses of human existence.

Lotus Sutra — A major scripture of Mahayana Buddhism containing countless examples of liberative techniques *(upāya)* used by the Buddha to deliver all beings.

Made to become so by itself (jinen) — A term favored by Shinran having several connotations: 1) transformation by the power of true compassion, 2) natural process of a person inevitably achieving supreme enlightenment, and 3) formless Buddhahood itself.

Mt. Hiei — Major monastic center of the Tendai school which produced the leading reformers of 13th-century Japan, including Hōnen, Shinran, Dōgen, Nichiren and others.

Name (myōgō) — The self articulation of reality, entering the world of human consciousness, as Namu-amida-butsu. Also referred to as the Name in six letters or six syllables.

Nara — Ancient capital of Japan during the Nara Period (710-784 C.E.); the center of the six schools of early Japanese Buddhism.

Nembutsu — The term is used variously in the Buddhist tradition. Originally, it meant contemplation on the Buddha, but in Pure Land Buddhism, it is used as follows: 1) recitation of the Name as the beckoning call from Amida Buddha, 2) self-articulation of reality informing human consciousness, and 3) fundamental cause of supreme enlightenment for a foolish being.

One Thought-moment (ichinen) — The instant when one awakens to the working of the Primal Vow, having been grasped never to be abandoned. That thought-moment is the instant of the self realization of reality when the timeless breaks through time. Since this is concretely realized in the saying of nembutsu, recitative nembutsu is referred to as the one-thought moment of practice.

One Vehicle — A key term in the Lotus Sutra which seeks to unify the diverse Buddhist paths into a single Vehicle. Shinran inherits this usage, but adds a Pure Land modifier and proclaims the Primal Vow of One Vehicle.

Other Power — The working of Amida's Primal Vow beyond the normal categories of subject and object, manifesting compassion which is the dynamic manifestation of 'sūnyatā (emptiness).

Path of Pure Land — The Pure Land tradition, open to all people regardless of class, gender, religiosity, etc., contrasted to the Path of Sages which is for the privileged few connected with the monastic institutions.

Practicer (gyōja) — The person who practices the Buddhist teaching in the midst of daily responsibilities earning a living, raising a family, meeting social obligations, etc. Everyday life is the *dōjō*, the training arena for wisdom and compassion.

Primal Vow (hongan) — The transcendental wish and prayer of the Buddha of Immeasurable Life and Light to bring all beings to supreme enlightenment, including the power to effect its successful realization in the midst of samsaric life.

Saichi (1851-1933) — An unlettered Shin devotee, who made a living making *geta* or wooden clogs. He left thousands of religious poems of unparalleled insights.

Self-power — The calculative mind of unenlightened beings who mistakenly believe in their ability to achieve supreme enlightenment. Relying on this delusion, the more they strive on the path, the more they sink into samsara.

Self-working — A form of calculative thinking based on self-power designs, hindering the working of the Primal Vow to effect transformation leading to supreme enlightenment.

Shan-tao (613-681) — One of the seven patriarchs of Shin Buddhism whose impact on Hōnen led to the establishment of an independent Pure Land School in 1175.

Shingon Esoterism — One of the major forms of Japanese Buddhism, centered on Mt. Kōya, during the rise of

Pure Land School in the 13th century.

Six Realms of Existence — The realms of hell, hungry ghosts, beasts, fighting demons, human beings, and heavenly beings, describing the different cycles of samsara.

T'an-luan (476-542) — The third patriarch of Shin Buddhism who made a major impact on the thought of Shinran.

Tathāgata — Literally, "thus-come" from the world of enlightenment to effect the salvation of all beings. Synonym of the Buddha, used in compound form as Amida Tathāgata (Amida Nyorai).

Ten Evils — Killing, stealing, adultery, lying, using harsh words, slandering, idle talk, greed, anger, and wrong views.

The Essentials of Faith Alone (Yuishinshō) — A tract written by Seikaku (1165-1235), a leading disciple of Honen. Shinran wrote a detailed explanation of key passages in his *Notes on Essentials of Faith Alone.*

Thirty-two Features and Eighty Characteristics — Ancient belief held in India that a superior being, such as a Buddha or World-conqueror, possesses special qualities which distinguished them from ordinary people.

Three Esoteric Practices — The Shingon training in body, mind, and speech that correspond with the cosmic Buddha's body, mind, and speech, attesting to the realization of supreme enlightenment. A secret training method, transmitted from master to disciple, hence, called esoteric.

True Entrusting (shinjin) — The core experience of Shin Buddhism in which a relative, finite being is made to entrust the self to Immeasurable Life and Light through the power of true compassion. Since it is not the calculative, self-power mind of sentient beings but the working of Other Power, it is indestructible; hence, it is likened to a diamond.

Wisdom of Non-origination — Wisdom that sees reality as-it-is, devoid of an abiding essence and frequently referred to as *'sūnyatā* (emptiness). As such, it does not appear or disappear in the conventional sense as seen by a deluded mind. This reality as-it-is is summed up in the phrase, "non-origination."

FOR FURTHER STUDY

Readers interested in a systematic study of Shinran's thought should consult *Shinran: An Introduction to His Life and Thought*, edited by Yoshifumi Ueda and Dennis Hirota (Kyoto: Hongwanji International Center, 1989). This work is based on the English translation of Shinran's writings published by the Hongwanji International Center under the general editorship of Ueda and a committee headed by Hirota. A list of the important works by Shinran which have been translated and published under the title, Hongwanji International Center Translation Series, is given below.

For a general survey of Shinran's life and thought the following works are suggested: *Shinran's Gospel of Pure Grace* by Alfred Bloom (Tucson: University of Arizona Press, 1965), *Shinran: His Life and Thought* by Norihiko Kikumura (Los Angeles: Nembutsu Press, 1972), and *Shinran and the Contemporary World*, edited by Nishi Hongwanji Commisson on the Promotion of Religious Education (Kyoto: Nishi Hongwanji, 1979). The list of secondary works of varying quality is now growing in number and information concerning them may be obtained by writing to either of the following addresses: 1) BCA Bookstore, 1710 Octavia Street, San Francisco, CA 94109, or 2) Office of Buddhist Education, Honpa Hongwanji Mission, 1727 Pali Highway, Honolulu, HI 96813.

Shinran's original works available in English translation under the auspices of the Hongwanji International Center are as follows:

The True Teaching, Practice, and Realization of the Pure Land Way (Kyōgyōshinshō). Volume I (1983), Volume II (1985), Volume III (1987), and Volume IV (1990).

Letters of Shinran (Mattoshō), 1978.

Notes on 'Essentials of Faith Alone' (Yuishinshō mon'i), 1979.

Notes on Once-calling and Many-calling (Ichinen-tanen mon'i), 1980.

Notes on Inscriptions on Sacred Scrolls (Songō shinzō meimon), 1981.

Passages on the Pure Land Way (Jōdo monrui jushō), 1983.

Hymns of the Pure Land (Jōdo wasan), 1991.

Another important collection of Shinran's works in English translation is found in the Ryukoku University Translation Series which has published the following works to date:

The Shōshinge (Gatha of True Faith in the Nembutsu), 1961.

Tannishō (Notes Lamenting Differences), 1962.

The Jōdo Wasan (The Hymns on the Pure Land), 1965.

The Kyō Gyō Shin Shō (The Teaching, Practice, Faith and Enlightenment), 1966. Selective translation.

The Kōsō Wasan (The Hymns on the Patriarchs), 1974.

Shōzōmatsu Wasan (The Hymns on the Last Age), 1980.

Most of the above works in both Series are available in either of the two Shin Buddhist bookstores in San Francisco and Honolulu, noted above.

Other Books About Shin Buddhism
from Buddhist Study Center Press

BUDDHA AND MAN
by Eikichi Ikeyama

This book has been skillfully translated from the original Japanese by Dr. Toshikazu Arai, an internationally oriented Buddhist writer. Nietzsche and Goethe were profound influences on Professor Ikeyama, who spent the early years of the twentieth century studying in Europe. His search for the meaning of Shin Buddhism in his own life was so intense that he subtitled this text, "Milestone."

ISBN 0-0938474-09-X   62 pages $8.95

SHOSHINGE: The Heart of Shin Buddhism
by Alfred Bloom

Alfred Bloom, one of the world's most beloved Buddhist scholars, writes in a clear, everyday style about the meaning and content of the sutra, Shoshinge, Shinran's thirteenth century poetic description of the origin, content, and joyful entrusting of what he saw as the ultimate insight of Mahayana Pure Land Buddhism.

ISBN 0-0938474-06-5   108 pages $8.95

LIVING SHIN BUDDHISM
by Ruth Tabrah

A deeply moving account of one of the twentieth century's most profound and direct nembutsu teachers. Rev. Masao Hanada gives the essence of Shinran's Shin Buddhist way through an account of how he himself became a truly human being. Second printing 1994.

ISBN 0-0938474-15-4   27 pages $2.95

TANNISHO, A Shin Buddhist Classic

Translated by Taitetsu Unno,
Professor of Religion at Smith College, Northampton, Massachusetts

Universities and colleges from coast to coast find this beautiful translation of one of Japan's most popular religious and literary classics a useful text in Comparative Religion, Buddhist Studies, Asian Studies and general multicultural courses in the Humanities. Dr. Unno, one of America's leading Shin Buddhist scholars, is an absorbing writer whose sensitive translation and accompanying commentary has also made this an extraordinarily popular book with Shin Buddhists everywhere.

ISBN 0-0938474-04-9 quality paper   **$8.95**

MEMOIRS OF A BUDDHIST WOMAN MISSIONARY IN HAWAII

by Shigeo Kikuchi

Both for those in women's studies and for Hawaiiana buffs, as well as for those curious about the role of a Buddhist missionary, these memoirs give a unique picture of rural life in early twentieth-century Hawaii. Wedding customs, the sending off to war of nisei boys in World War I, the cooperative nature of life in an early plantation community, and the fortitude of a woman missionary living on the edge of poverty, are portrayed with the author's Buddhist focus which enabled her to live through the most difficult conditions with inner strength and serenity.

ISBN 0-0938474-13-8   **73 pages $8.95**

THE BUDDHIST WORLD OF AWAKENING

by Takamaro Shigaraki

A clear and incisive exploration of Shin Buddhism (Jodo Shinshu) that is widely used in colleges and universities offering courses in Asian studies, Buddhist studies, or Comparative Religion. The freshness of Shigaraki's approach has also drawn a large general readership. This book has recently been translated into German and Polish.

ISBN 0-0938474-02-2   **86 pages $8.95**

Other Books About Shin Buddhism
from Buddhist Study Center Press

AN INTRODUCTION TO SHIN BUDDHISM
by T. Shigaraki

A paper bound booklet that is exactly what the title implies: a brief analysis of the role of religion in modern life and the nature of Shin Buddhism as contemporary religious focus. Also available in large print.

ISBN 0-0938474-11-1   **$2.95**

THE PATH OF AWAKENING
by Kosho Soga

A collection of dharma talks for everyday life, of special appeal to those in their twenties and thirties. The author, who is in that age group himself, writes in a powerful way about the meaning of Shin Buddhism in this modern, scientific, nuclear age. Confronted by the deaths of a young cousin and a beloved grandfather, he comes to an understanding and personal acceptance of the religious path he earlier rejected.

ISBN 0-0938474-07-3   **63 pages $8.95**

BODHISATTVAS EVERYWHERE
by T. Sakakibara, translated by T. Arai

A moving account of what one perceptive Buddhist teacher sees as the reality of his life as a soldier in China, a husband left with an infant child to raise, a priest torn between tradition and his yearning to live a meaningful life. Reflections in the setting of 1000 year old Jojuji temple in the hills above Kyoto, cover the wide range of Sakakibara's thoughts on education, violence, genetic engineering, and how it is that he sees bodhisattvas everywhere.

ISBN 0-0938474-03-0   **63 pages $8.95**

RESOURCE FOR MODERN LIVING: TANNISHO
by Alfred Bloom

A few copies of this first edition of Alfred Bloom's bestselling existential interpretation of the Shin Buddhist classic Tannisho are still available.

ISBN 0-0938474-00-6   quality paper   **102 pages $8.95**

Other Books About Shin Buddhism
from **Buddhist Study Center Press**

ONE MAN'S JOURNEY,
A Spiritual Autobiography
by Kazuo Miyamoto

A rich reflection on living in the worlds of East and West by a Honolulu physician who experienced and appreciated both. The candor and sensitivity of this Hawaii-born, mainland educated nisei, his deep Buddhist commitment and his vivid writing style appeal to readers young and old. Now in second printing.

ISBN 0-0938474-04-9   120 pages   **$8.95**

AJATASATRU:
THE STORY OF WHO WE ARE
by Shoji Matsumoto and Ruth Tabrah

This is the first easy-to-read translation of the Nirvana sutra episode relating the ancient tragedy of a son murdering his father, and searching for a way to live with what he regrets having done. This story is timeless, an historic incident in which modern men and women can find everything they want to know about themselves, about human nature and the compassion and wisdom of the Buddha. A new century sutra is how the authors view this third section of Shinran's master text, *Kyo-Gyo-Shin-Sho.*

ISBN 0-0938474-07-3   **71 pages $8.95**

SHIN SUTRAS TO LIVE BY
A new century publication edited by
Ruth Tabrah and Shoji Matsumoto

Modern English translations of the three basic sutras of Shin Buddhism: *Shoshinge, Sanbutsuge* and *Juseige* plus an explanation of the meaning and value of sutra chanting, a translation of eko, and a new century homage. A basic English language resource of Shin Buddhist ritual.

ISBN 0-0938474-12-X   paper   **45 pages $5.95**
Also available on audio cassette   **$2.95**

THE NATURAL WAY
OF SHIN BUDDHISM

by Shoji Matsumoto and Ruth Tabrah

This book takes the reader on a fascinating journey into how Buddhism began in India 2500 years ago, the teaching of Amida Buddha on which Pure Land Buddhism is based, and the way in which the thirteenth century poet and teacher Shinran opened a new horizon in Mahayana Buddhism. Both for those encountering Pure Land Buddhist thought for the first time, and those for whom it has been an inherited tradition, this book provides a contemporary view of Shinran's creative insights and their potential for men and women seeking a meaningful, nondiscriminating, scientifically compatible, non-theistic religious focus. Reviewer George Gatenby says this is a "book by people who clearly live the way they describe and delight in a treasure to all who own it, a resource to return to many times."

ISBN 0-938474-14-6   **176 pages**   **$9.95**

═══════════ *Available from:* ═══════════

BUDDHIST STUDY CENTER PRESS
1727 Pali Highway
Honolulu, Hawaii 96813 USA

Telephone: (808) 522-9210 • Fax: (808) 522-9209